GOVERNMENT TODAY
WORKBOOK

by
Beverly Vaillancourt

The Peoples Publishing Group, Inc
Free to Learn, to Grow, to Change

1-800-822-1080

Editorial Manager, Bonnie Diamond, Ed.D.
Pre-Press & Production Manager, Doreen E. Smith
Electronic Design, Eric Grajo
Cover Design, Jeremy Mayes
Electronic Page Production, Kristine Liebman
Copy Editor, Proofreader, Christine Cannistraro

ISBN 1-56-256-037-9

TABLE OF CONTENTS

TABLE OF CONTENTS

(continued)

FOCUS

Why is government needed? _____

_____

_____

_____

_____

_____

A Complete each sentence with a word from the box. Write your answer in the space provided.

democracy	dictatorship	monarchy	communism

1. The form of government in China is called _____ .

2. In a _____ , people vote for their leaders.

3. In a _____ , one person has unlimited power in government.

4. A form of government that has a ruling family is called a _____ .

5. Under _____ , people have few freedoms.

6. A form of government in which the people have a vote is a _____ .

7. People have few rights in a _____ . One person holds all the power.

8. Kings and queens are the government leaders in a _____ .

9. The people of China wanted to change from _____ to a _____ .

10. People do not vote for their leaders under communism, or in a _____ .

B Answer each of the following questions in a complete sentence.

How does a country's form of government affect its people? _____

_____

_____

How is a monarchy different from a democracy? _____

_____

_____

FOCUS

Why do you think democracy in America has worked for over 200 years? _____

_____

_____

_____

_____

Complete the outline below by writing each fact in the box under the correct heading. Some facts will be listed under both headings. Some lines may be left blank.

all people have a say in new laws	used by state governments
used by local governments	representatives speak for the people
the people elect their law-makers	often used by small groups such as clubs
majority rules	also called a republic

I. Direct Democracy

   A. _____

   B. _____

   C. _____

   D. _____

   E. _____

   F. _____

   G. _____

II. Representative Democracy

   A. _____

   B. _____

   C. _____

   D. _____

   E. _____

   F. _____

   G. _____

FOCUS

Why do you think the colonists wanted to be able to govern themselves? _____

_____

_____

_____

_____

A Place the events listed in the correct place on the time line. Write the letter of the event in the space provided.

Native Americans are forced to move west

King George rules the colonies

People come to America from other parts of Europe

The Jamestown colony begins

b.   100 people sail for America from Europe

d.   King James sends a governor to Jamestown

f.   The London Company lets Jamestown set up its own government

| 1606 | 1607 | 1619 | 1624 | 1700's | |

B Answer the following questions in complete sentences.

Did King James agree that Jamestown should have its own form of government? Explain.

_____

Why did people come to America from Europe? _____

_____

How did people coming to America affect the country? _____

_____

How did the growth of the colonies change government in America? _____

_____

FOCUS

Is a limited democracy better than no democracy at all?

Explain. _____

_____

_____

_____

_____

A Read each statement. If the statement is true, write **T** on the line. Write **F** if the statement is false.

_____ 1. Town meetings were the main form of government in the Southern colonies.

_____ 2. Under King James, the colonies were ruled by an English monarchy.

_____ 3. Indentured servants worked for seven years for no pay.

_____ 4. Most colonists wanted to pay taxes to England.

_____ 5. England wanted the colonists to have a representative government.

_____ 6. Some colonists wanted England to rule the colonies while others did not.

_____ 7. The phrase "No taxation without representation" meant that someone in the government should collect taxes.

_____ 8. The Sugar Act required the colonists to pay a duty on all products made of paper.

B Five of the statements above are false. Rewrite each false statement to make it true. Reread Lesson 4 if you need help.

1. _____

_____

2. _____

_____

3. _____

_____

4. _____

_____

5. _____

_____

FOCUS

Which point of the Declaration of Independence do you think is the most important? Why? _____

_____

_____

_____

A Read the sentences. Place the events in the order in which they happened by writing the letters **a** (first) through **g** (last) in the spaces provided.

_____ a. The First Continental Congress met in Philadelphia

_____ b. The colonies became known as the United States of America

_____ c. The battle at Concord

_____ d. The colonists fought the American Revolution

_____ e. The Articles of Confederation were written to limit the power of a central government

_____ f. The Second Continental Congress passed the Declaration of Independence

_____ g. The colonies formed a confederation

B Use what you have learned in Lessons 1-5 to answer the following question. Write your answer in paragraph form using at least three complete sentences.

Why do you think the Articles of Confederation did not allow for a President for the country? What problems do you think resulted? _____

_____

_____

_____

_____

_____

_____

_____

_____

FOCUS

The delegates who met to rewrite the Articles of Confederation met in secret. Why do you think men planning a democracy would do so in secret? _____

_____

_____

_____

A Match each term in *Column B* with its description in *Column A*. Write the letter of the correct term in the space provided.

Column A	Column B
_____ 1. government by a ruling family	a. Northwest Ordinance
_____ 2. agreement to count some slaves as part of the population	b. American Revolution
_____ 3. set up a central government	c. Three-fifths Compromise
_____ 4. one person who controls all of the government	d. delegate
_____ 5. a representative form of government	e. the Great Compromise
_____ 6. replaced the Articles of Confederation	f. Articles of Confederation
_____ 7. set up two Houses in the government	g. debt
_____ 8. representative, or person, who speaks for others	h. democracy
_____ 9. money owed to others	i. monarchy
_____ 10. the number of people living in an area	j. the Constitution
	k. population
	l. dictator

B Circle the word in parentheses that makes each sentence correct.

1. The Articles of Confederation set up a (weak/strong) central government.

2. The Articles of Confederation was replaced by the (Three-fifths Compromise/Constitution).

3. The Southern states wanted to (count/not count) enslaved African Americans as part of their population.

4. The Great Compromise set up the Senate and the (House of Representatives/Congress).

5. To ratify means to (agree/disagree) with.

FOCUS

Do you think federal laws should always be "supreme?" Why or why not?_____

_____

_____

_____

_____

A | Show how the Constitution sets up the federal government.

Constitution

Branch

Made Up of

Purpose

B | Explain each of the following ideas in the chart below.

Separation of power	
Checks and balances	
Popular sovereignty	
Limited government	

FOCUS

Could a democracy exist without freedom of speech? Explain.

_____

_____

_____

_____

A Write the number of the amendment that deals with each right listed below. Use the Bill of Rights on page 23 of your textbook if you need help.

_____ a. rights of states

_____ b. freedom of speech

_____ c. right to a speedy trial

_____ d. right to keep arms

_____ e. freedom of religion

_____ f. right to a jury trial

_____ g. protection from unreasonable search or seizure

_____ h. protection from unfair punishment

_____ i. the right to assemble

_____ j. freedom of the press

_____ k. people not forced to house soldiers

_____ l. rights beyond the Constitution

B Choose the word or term from the box that best completes each sentence. Write your answer in the space provided.

amendment	freedom	jury
supreme	Bill of Rights	ratify
liberty	petition	

1. The _____ lists the basic freedoms of U.S. citizens.

2. Another word for freedom is _____ .

3. A right is a basic _____ .

4. An _____ is a change made to the Constitution.

5. Each state was asked to _____ the Bill of Rights.

6. A group of people chosen to hear and decide on a court case is called a _____.

FOCUS

Which amendments affect you the most? _____

_____

_____

_____

_____

A List Amendments 11-27 by number under the correct heading below.

Rights of the People	Rights of the State

Powers of Congress	Ways the federal government is organized

B Choose two questions asked in Lesson 9 of the text. Answer each question. Support each answer with good reasons.

_____

_____

_____

_____

_____

_____

_____

FOCUS

How does not being able to read keep someone from exercising his or her voting rights? _____

_____

_____

_____

Circle the letter of the word or phrase that best completes each statement.

1. Voting in 1791 was limited to _____ .

   a. soldiers   b. free, white males   c. all adults

2. The writers of the Constitution left voting rights up to the _____ .

   a. states   b. Bill of Rights   c. President

3. The Fifteenth Amendment gave the vote to _____ .

   a. everyone   b. adult men and women   c. adult male citizens

4. Money paid to vote is called a _____ .

   a. poll tax   b. ballot fee   c. literacy ticket

5. The last people given the right to vote were _____ .

   a. women   b. people ages 18 to 20   c. Native Americans

6. Women were given the right to vote in _____ .

   a. 1870   b. 1920   c. 1971

7. The _____ Amendment gave people ages 18 through 20 the right to vote.

   a. Fourteenth   b. Twenty-sixth   c. Twenty-ninth

8. Native Americans were given the right to vote in _____ .

   a. 1791   b. 1920   c. 1924

9. The _____ Amendment gave African American men over age 20 the right to vote.

   a. Fifteenth   b. Nineteenth   c. Twenty-sixth

10. The war that helped women gain the right to vote was _____ .

   a. World War I   b. World War II   c. Vietnam

FOCUS

What is a civil right? _____

_____

_____

_____

_____

_____

A Answer each of the following questions in a complete sentence.

What are two civil rights you enjoy? _____

_____

_____

_____

How do these two rights affect your life? _____

_____

_____

_____

What other civil rights do you feel you should have? Explain. _____

_____

B Use the information given in Lesson 11 to fill in each box. Write the name of the law.

Laws that limited civil rights	Laws that expanded civil rights
_____	_____
_____	_____
_____	_____
_____	_____
_____	_____

FOCUS

Do you feel that the use of electors is a fair way to elect the President and the Vice President? Explain. _____

_____

_____

_____

_____

A Read each statement. If the statement is true, write **T** on the line. Write **F** if the stateme is false.

_____ 1. A President and a Vice President are elected every four years.

_____ 2. The President is elected by only a vote of the people.

_____ 3. Electors are people who help voters vote.

_____ 4. The person running for President chooses the candidate for Vice President.

_____ 5. Only people born in the United States may run for President.

_____ 6. In the past, voting was limited to white males who were married.

_____ 7. A person may live outside the United States and still run for President.

_____ 8. Campaigning for President costs a lot of money.

_____ 9. The President and Vice President run as a team.

_____ 10. The President and Vice President are elected by the electoral vote.

B Four of the statements above are false. Rewrite each false statement to make it true. Reread Lesson 12 if you need help.

1. _____

_____

2. _____

_____

3. _____

_____

4. _____

_____

FOCUS

Why do you think the President and Vice President are elected as a team? _____

_____

_____

_____

_____

A List five qualities of a good Vice President.

_____

_____

_____

_____

_____

B Answer each of the following questions in a complete sentence.

Who is the Vice President today? _____

How long has this person been Vice President? _____

Who is the President today? _____

Do you think the current Vice President would make a good President? Why or why not? _____

_____

What other powers do you think would be good for the Vice President to have? _____

_____

_____

C Check an encyclopedia for information about U.S. Presidents. Make a list of 5 Vice Presidents who were later elected as President.

_____   3. _____   5. _____

_____   4. _____

More About Elections

Do you feel an open or closed primary is better? Why? _____

_____

_____

_____

_____

A Write each of the steps in the election process in one of the boxes below.

a. primary elections

d. political party
   convention

b. Inauguration Day

e. campaign

c. electoral vote

f. popular vote

The Steps in the Election Process of a President

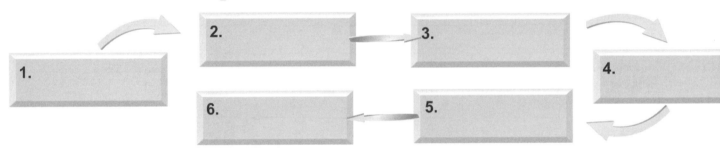

1.

2.

3.

4.

5.

6.

B Fill in each blank to complete the sentence.

1. Since 1951, a President may serve only _____ terms.

2. A President is elected every _____ years.

3. Franklin D. Roosevelt was elected to _____ terms as President.

4. The _____ Amendment states that a President can be in office for only two terms.

5. There are _____ kinds of primary elections.

6. Today, primary elections are held in _____ states.

7. Each President and Vice President serve a _____ - year term.

8. Inauguration Day is January _____.

FOCUS

How can the support of a political party help a candidate run for office? _____

_____

_____

_____

_____

Answer each of the following questions in a complete sentence.

What is the difference between a major and minor political party? _____

_____

_____

What are the two major political parties in the United States? _____

_____

_____

What affect can minor parties have on an election? _____

_____

_____

What is a third-party candidate? _____

_____

_____

Create your own political party. Name your party. Write a paragraph stating your party's platform.

Party Name _____

_____

_____

_____

_____

_____

FOCUS

What qualities make a good Chief Executive? _____

_____

_____

_____

_____

A Circle the letter of the word or phrase that best completes each statement.

1. The President is the head of the _____ .

   a. Constitution   b. Executive Office   c. impeachment office

2. The President may issue _____ .

   a. an executive order   b. new laws   c. a judicial review

3. A President may be _____ .

   a. impeached   b. appointed   c. an advisor

4. Cabinet members are the heads of _____ .

   a. budget agencies   b. federal departments   c. security councils

5. Cabinet members are chosen by _____ .

   a. the Chief of Staff   b. the Vice President   c. the President

6. The _____ Amendment says what happens when the President must leave office.

   a. Nineteenth   b. Twenty-second   c. Twenty-fifth

7. If a President becomes ill or dies while in office, the _____ takes over.

   a. Vice President   b. Chief of Staff   c. electoral college

8. The _____ sets up the President's day.

   a. Vice President   b. Chief of Staff   c. Cabinet member

9. The Executive Office of the President is run from the _____ .

   a. Management Office   b. National Security Council   c. White House

10. A plan for spending and collecting money is called _____ .

    a. an agency   b. an office   c. a budget

FOCUS

Why is the State of the Union Address one of the President's most important speeches? _____

_____

_____

_____

A *cause* makes something happen. What happens is the *effect*. Complete each cause with an effect.

Cause	Effect
The President vetoes a bill	1. _____
The President signs a bill	2. _____
The President gives the State of the Union address	3. _____
The President calls a special session of Congress	4. _____

Write a definition for each term in your own words.

veto _____

_____

bill _____

_____

policy _____

_____

treaty _____

_____

legislator _____

_____

session _____

FOCUS

What is the most important job of the President as the Chief Diplomat? _____

_____

_____

_____

_____

A Circle the word or phrase that makes each sentence correct.

1. A person who represents a country when dealing with other countries is a (delegate/diplomat).

2. The way one country deals with another country is its (military/foreign) policy.

3. A written agreement between two or more countries is a (treaty/canal).

4. A treaty made by the President must be approved by (Congress/the military).

5. A person who represents his or her country in other countries is called (a foreigner/ an ambassador).

6. An ambassador is one kind of (diplomat/legislator).

7. People who work as ambassadors for the United States are chosen by (Congress/the President).

8. President (Carter/Nixon) agreed to a treaty with the government of China in 1981.

B Read the paragraph. Write what happened in you own words. Then discuss how Preside Carter acted as the Chief Diplomat of the United States

For many years governments of Israel and Egypt did not agree. Battles over land were often fought. In 1978, President Carter invited President Anwar al-Sadat of Egypt and Prime Minister Menachem Begin of Israel to the United States. He worked with them to bring peace between the two countries. In 1979, Sada and Begin signed the first peace treaty between Israel and an Arab country.

1. What happened? _____

_____

2. How did President Carter act as Chief Diplomat? _____

_____

FOCUS

Why do you think the framers of America's government did not give the President the power to declare war? _____

_____

_____

_____

_____

A Place a check mark (✔) in the box beside each duty the President has as Commander in Chief.

1. directs war efforts

2. heads the armed forces

3. can declare war

4. can order troops to fight a war for 75 days

5. can limit civil rights during a war

☐ 6. sets up a budget for the armed forces

☐ 7. picks the leaders of the armed forces

☐ 8. can place limits on prices during war

☐ 9. decides where the armed forces will be in the world

☐10. can limit the sale of food during a war

B List three facts about the War Powers Act.

_____

_____

_____

_____

_____

_____

C Use what you know about the War Powers Act to write your opinion below.

How long should the President have to wait to go to war before getting an okay from Congress?

_____

_____

FOCUS

As President, what would you think about before deciding who to appoint as a federal judge? _____

_____

_____

_____

_____

Read the list of duties. List each duty under the correct heading in the chart. Reread Lessons 13 through 17 if you need help.

a. signs a bill into law

b. heads the armed forces

c. appoints Cabinet members

d. grants pardons

e. directs war efforts

f. appoints federal judges

g. sets up foreign policy

h. can veto a bill

i. signs treaties

j. appoints ambassadors

k. appoints the heads of federal agencies

l. enforces federal laws

m. sets up the federal budget

n. can limit freedoms during times of war

Duties of the President of the United States

1. Chief Executive	
2. Chief Legislator	
3. Chief Jurist	
4. Chief Diplomat	
5. Commander in Chief	

FOCUS

Should cabinet members be elected or appointed? Why? _____

_____

_____

_____

_____

_____

Choose the word from the box that best completes each sentence. Write your choice in the space provided. Three words will not be used.

~~binet~~	secretaries	term	Commerce
~~partments~~	Vice President	Labor	appointed
~~torney General~~	War	elected	
~~ustice~~	advisors	members	

Congress set up three executive (1) _____ in 1789 to help President Washington run the government. The names of these three departments were the Department of State, the Department of (2) _____ and the Department of the Treasury. The office of the (3) _____ was also set up to advise the President about laws and to help the President enforce the laws of the country.

The people who head the executive departments are called (4) _____. As a group, all of the President's advisors make up the (5) _____. The (6) _____ of the United States is also a part of Cabinet meetings.

The people who make up the Cabinet are (7) _____ to their jobs by the President. Usually, the job of a Cabinet member ends when the President's (8) _____ in office ends. Sometimes, a new President will keep a Cabinet member from the past president's Cabinet. Three names of executive departments are (9)_____, (10)_____, (11)_____.

The Department of State

How does the need for oil from the countries of the Middle East affect the United States foreign policy toward these countries? _____

_____

_____

_____

A Complete each sentence with a word that makes the sentence correct.

1. The _____ heads the Department of State.

2. _____ can be used by a country to try to force a change in the country's foreign policies.

3. The way one country deals with other countries is called _____ .

4. _____ are given to people who wish to travel to foreign countries.

5. The Department of State advises the President on the _____ of other countries.

6. The Department of State is part of the _____ branch of government.

7. The Secretary of State answers directly to the _____ .

8. A _____ allows a person to live and to work in a foreign country.

9. Diplomatic offices called _____ help American citizens traveling in foreign countries.

10. An _____ represents the foreign policy of the United States while living in a foreign country.

B Use the Internet or library reference book to answer the following questions.

1. Who is the Secretary of State now? _____

_____

2. Which President appointed the person who is now the Secretary of State? _____

_____

FOCUS

Do you think women soldiers should have to meet the same physical standards set for male soldiers? Why or why not? ____

_____

_____

_____

_____

A Use the terms in the box to complete the chart below.

Secretary of the Army	Secretary of the Air Force	Chairperman of the Joint Chiefs
Secretary of the Marines	Secretary of Defense	of Staff
Secretary of the Navy		

Department of Defense Chain of Command

President of the United States

B Write a short essay about the U.S. military draft. Finish by stating your opinion. Back up your opinion with reasons. Use another piece of paper if you need to.

_____

_____

_____

FOCUS

What changes to public buildings assist people with special physical needs? _____

_____

_____

_____

_____

A List the four jobs of the Department of Justice.

1. _____

2. _____

3. _____

4. _____

B Complete the chart below. Write the names of four divisions. List the main job of each division in the box below the division.

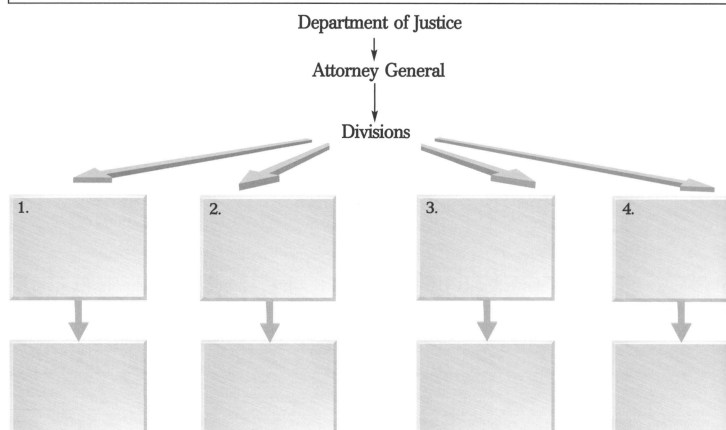

Department of Justice

↓

Attorney General

↓

Divisions

1.

2.

3.

4.

Use with Lesson

FOCUS

What problems can occur when trying to count the people living in the United States? _____

_____

_____

_____

_____

A Circle the letter of the word or phrase that best completes each statement.

The Department of Commerce gives out _____ .

a. passports   b. patents   c. unemployment

Every ten years the Department of Commerce takes a _____ .

a. census   b. rural   c. patent

The term commerce means _____ .

a. economy   b. welfare   c. trade

A census is a count of the _____ of an area.

a. economy   b. population   c. patents

A patent gives someone the right to own _____ .

a. an invention's design b. product standards c. trade agreements

B Use the U.S. Population 1790–1990 chart in the Data Bank. Create a line graph for both the rural and urban populations.

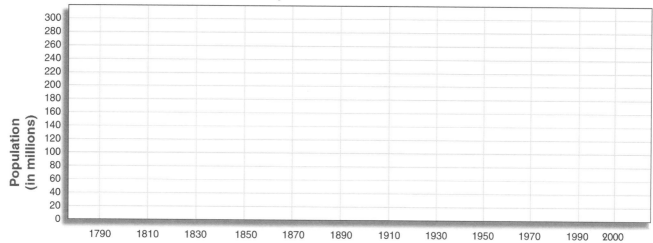

U.S. Population 1790–2000

The Department of Labor

Why do you think the Department of Labor is so concerned with worker safety? _____

_____

_____

_____

_____

Read the rules from the *Fair Labor Standards Act of 1938*. Answer the questions below.

Type of Work	Minimum Age	Maximum Hours
Nonfarm work	16	
Deliver paper, gather evergreens, perform on TV, radio, or stage, work in parents' business	any age	
Any nonhazardous job for unlimited hours	age 16 and 17	
Nonhazardous job for limited hours	age 14 and 15	• 3 hours on school days • 18 hours in school week • 8 hours on nonschool day • 40 hours in nonschool week • 7:00 A.M.-7:00 P.M. school term • 7:00 A.M.-9:00 P.M. June 1-Labor Day

1. Name 3 jobs and the hours a 15-year-old can work.

   a. _____

   b. _____

   c. _____

2. Name 3 jobs you can do.

   a. _____

   b. _____

   c. _____

3. Set up a weekly schedule for work and school on a separate paper. List the days of the week across the top of the page. List the hours of the day along the left.

FOCUS

How does the work of the Department of Agriculture affect us every day? _____

_____

_____

_____

_____

Read this paragraph. Then answer each question below in a complete sentence.

In 1997, *Hudson Foods of Nebraska*, a meat packaging plant, was forced to close. Hudson Foods made hamburger patties for many companies. Inspectors from the Department of Agriculture found *E. coli* in the meat. *E. coli* is a dangerous bacteria. It can make people very ill. At least twenty people who had eaten the meat at fast food restaurants became very sick. Hudson Foods could not reopen their plant until the Department of Agriculture felt the food was safe. Hudson Foods had to destroy much of the meat it had processed. This cost the company a great deal of money. In the end, Hudson Foods sold the meat packaging plant.

Why did Hudson Foods close? _____

_____

_____

What role did the Department of Agriculture play in the closing of Hudson Foods? _____

_____

_____

Why was the plant sold? _____

_____

_____

FOCUS

What does the Department of the Interior do? _____

_____

_____

_____

_____

A Look up Yellowstone National Park in an encyclopedia. Then fill in the chart below.

Yellowstone National Park

1.	Found in which 3 states	
2.	Size (square mi. or km)	
3.	Found in which chain of mountains	
4.	Highest mountain elevation	
5.	Famous geyser	
6.	River in park	
7.	Year it became national park	

B Write a paragraph about Yellowstone National Park below.

_____

_____

_____

_____

_____

FOCUS

What does the Department of Energy do? _____

_____

_____

_____

_____

Answer each of the following questions in a complete sentence.

How does the Department of Energy affect you?

a. _____

b. _____

c. _____

What is the current price of gasoline in your area? _____

What was the price of gasoline last month? _____

What do you think the price of gasoline will be next month? _____

How do you think events in the Middle East affect gasoline prices in the United States? _____

_____

What source of energy is used to heat your school? _____

_____

What is one way you could save energy? _____

_____

Wind and solar energy are two other sources of energy. Draw a design below using wind or solar energy as an energy source.

What are the jobs of the Department of the Treasury? _____

_____

_____

_____

_____

_____

Read this paragraph. Then write your *opinion* to the questions in complete sentences.

In 1998, Congress gave the U.S. Treasury Department the okay to begin minting dollar coins. These coins can be used instead of dollar bills. It costs about 8¢ to make a coin. It costs about half that to mint a bill. Yet, the U.S. Treasury Department believes this will save U.S. taxpayers about $100 million over five years.

Americans once used a dollar coin called the Susan B. Anthony dollar. It was not well-liked. The new dollar coin is gold in color and is similar in size to a quarter.

1. Do you think Americans will use dollar coins? Why or why not? _____

_____

_____

2. Do you think minting dollar coins is a good idea? Why or why not? _____

_____

_____

3. Whose picture do you think should be on the coin? Explain your answer. _____

_____

_____

4. What advice would you give to the Department of the Treasury? _____

_____

_____

The Department of Health and Human Services

FOCUS

What is social security? _____

_____

_____

_____

_____

A | Place a check mark (✔) in each box next to a phrase that describes a job of the Department of Health and Human Services.

1. directs health programs

2. gives out food stamps

3. watches over food safety

4. pays social security benefits

5. helps people who are blind to pay for their living costs

6. sets worker safety rules

☐ 7. gives out passports

☐ 8. helps the aged to pay their living costs

☐ 9. tracks the spread of diseases

☐ 10. sets policy for federal lands

☐ 11. helps people who are disabled to pay for their living costs

☐ 12. says which drugs can be sold

B | Write a paragraph comparing the Department of Health and Human Services with the Department of Labor. How are they alike? How do they differ?

_____

_____

_____

_____

_____

_____

_____

_____

_____

_____

The Department of Education

FOCUS

Which areas of education are most important to fund? _____

_____

_____

_____

_____

_____

Context Clue Words

Words that Hint Definitions	Words that Hint Comparisons	Words that Hint More Information
meaning or means	some or other	and, also, too, much, many
for example	sometimes, other times	in addition or in addition to,
called, or	like, different from	finally
known as	however, but, yet	next

A Use the information in the box to identify what the context clues in the sentences belo hint. Write the term definition, comparison, or more information in the space provided beside each statement.

_____ 1. Schools set up to educate all individuals are known as public schools.

_____ 2. In addition to the seventeen states that had segregated schools in 1954, there were many local governments who had segregated schools.

_____ 3. In a case called *Brown v. the Board of Education of Topeka, Kansas* the U.S. Supreme Court ruled that "separate but equal" was not equal.

_____ 4. A next step in vocational, or job-training, programs offered is to make sure that training for the 21st century occurs.

_____ 5. Sometimes public schools offer bilingual classes.

B On a separate sheet of paper, write a brief essay that states your opinion about the following question: What are the benefits of a good education?

Use with Lesso

FOCUS

What does the Department of Housing and Urban Development do? _____

_____

_____

_____

A Read the phrases below in *Column A*. Write each phrase in *Column B* to show the correct order of events leading to the start of The Department of Housing and Urban Development.

Column A	*Column B*
people move from the rural areas to the cities	1
HUD sets up funds for public housing	2
twelve million people move to the United States	3
housing becomes a major problem	4

B Write your opinion to these questions in complete sentences.

How can low-income housing be improved? How can government help? _____

_____

_____

_____

Should U.S. taxpayers pay flood relief to people whose homes are along coast lines or in

areas that easily flood? Why or why not? _____

_____

FOCUS

What transportation rules does the Department of Transportation set up? _____

_____

_____

_____

_____

A List seven jobs of The Department of Transportation.

1. _____   5. _____

2. _____   6. _____

3. _____   7. _____

4. _____

B Explain three ways the Department of Transportation affects you.

1. _____

2. _____

3. _____

C Read these airline travel rules. Then write a reason why you think the rules exist.

Airline Rule	Reason for Rule
1. overbook or sell more seats than plane has	a. _____
2. accept wheelchairs as baggage	b. _____
3. do not allow smoking on flights shorter than 6 hours	c. _____
4. offer a free flight coupon to someone who loses his or her seat because of overbooking	d. _____
5. give free hotel room and meals to a person who loses a seat because of overbooking	e. _____

FOCUS

In what ways should the United States government help veterans? _____

_____

_____

_____

_____

A Read each sentence. If the sentence is a fact, write **F** in the space provided. If the statement is an opinion, write **O**.

_____ 1. The Department of Veterans Affairs was set up in 1989.

_____ 2. The Department of Veterans Affairs first concern should be victims of combat shock.

_____ 3. Agent Orange had to be used in Vietnam.

_____ 4. The budget for the Department of Veterans Affairs should be more than $50 billion.

_____ 5. The Department of Veterans Affairs has special care homes for veterans.

_____ 6. Many soldiers who came into contact with Agent Orange have developed life-long illnesses.

_____ 7. Veterans of the Vietnam War should get more money than veterans of other wars.

_____ 8. Soldiers who fought in the Revolutionary War were paid in cash and land.

_____ 9. Too much money is spent on medical care for veterans who did not get hurt while in combat.

_____ 10. All veterans should be given free medical care, no matter what is wrong with them.

B List seven jobs of the Department of Veterans Affairs.

_____   5. _____

_____   6. _____

_____   7. _____

_____

FOCUS

Should the EPA become an executive department? Why or why not? _____
_____
_____
_____
_____
_____

A

Classify each agency listed as a service agency or a regulatory agency by writing its name in the correct column of the table.

Environmental Protection Agency
National Aeronautics and Space Administration
Federal Deposit Insurance Corporation
Interstate Commerce Commission

Consumer Product Safety Commission
Federal Trade Commission
U.S. Postal Service
Federal Reserve Board

Service Agencies	Regulatory Agencies

B

Write the name of each government office for each abbreviation below.

1. NASA _____

2. EPA _____

3. FDIC _____

4. CPSC _____

5. CIA _____

6. USPS _____

7. FBI _____

8. DOE _____

9. INS _____

10. FCC _____

11. DOT _____

12. FAA _____

FOCUS

Where can you find information about how to get a civil service job? _____

_____

_____

_____

_____

A Read each statement. If the statement is true, write **T** on the line. Write **F** if the statement if false.

_____ 1. The United States Postal Service employs more than 800,000 people.

_____ 2. Most jobs with the federal government are outside of Washington, D.C.

_____ 3. People with civil service jobs cannot work for the federal government.

_____ 4. The U.S. government is the smallest employer in the country.

_____ 5. The many offices that make up the government are called a bureaucracy.

_____ 6. Civil service workers are not allowed to join labor unions.

_____ 7. At one time, all civil service jobs were appointed.

_____ 8. The Civil Rights Commission is a federal agency that is concerned with making sure everyone's civil rights are protected.

_____ 9. The Civil Rights Act set up the civil service.

_____ 10. Many of the top jobs in the government are not civil service jobs.

B Four of the statements above are false. Rewrite each false statement to make it true.

_____

_____

_____

_____

_____

_____

_____

_____

FOCUS

Is it good for both the President and the majority in Congress to be from the same political party? Explain. _____

_____

_____

_____

_____

Reread Lesson 34. Find the main idea of each bold heading. Write the main idea from each section. Add details to your main idea.

34.1 _____

_____

_____

_____

34.2 _____

_____

_____

_____

34.3 _____

_____

_____

_____

34.4 _____

_____

_____

_____

34.5 _____

_____

_____

FOCUS

What do you think would be a reason to "censure" a member of Congress? _____

_____

_____

_____

_____

A Complete the chart by writing the missing information in the spaces provided.

	Length of Term	Qualifications	Number in House
Senators			
Representatives			

B Fill in each blank to best complete the sentence.

The results of the census divide each state into _____ .

The number of _____ in each state is equal to the number of districts.

The First Article of the Constitution says representatives are to be elected by a

_____ election.

The _____ Amendment calls for the direct election of senators.

A state may gain or lose a representative if its population _____ .

C Answer the question below in a complete sentence.

How do the qualifications to hold office for a senator differ from those for a representative?_____

_____

_____

The Powers of Congress

Who stopped the ERA from becoming the 27th Amendment?

_____

_____

_____

_____

_____

A Read each statement. If the statement is true, write **T** on the line. Write **F** if the stateme is false.

_____ 1. Congress has the power to tax citizens.

_____ 2. Only Congress may declare war.

_____ 3. Amendments passed using the legislative method do not leave Congress.

_____ 4. Congress is given implied powers by the Constitution.

_____ 5. Laws written by Congress affect the whole country.

_____ 6. The elastic clause gives Congress expressed powers.

_____ 7. In 1972, the Equal Rights Amendment became part of the Constitution.

_____ 8. The Twenty-first Amendment lets states decide their own laws for selling alcoholic drinks.

_____ 9. Setting up federal courts is not a power given to Congress.

_____ 10. Congress is given expressed powers in Article I of the Constitution.

B Four of the statements above are false. Rewrite each false statement to make it true.

1. _____

   _____

2. _____

   _____

3. _____

   _____

4. _____

   _____

FOCUS

Why do you think about one-third of the bills sent to Congress are signed into law? _____

_____

_____

_____

_____

Circle the letter of the word or phrase that best completes each statement.

1. A proposed law is called _____ .

   a. an implied power   b. a bill   c. a veto

2. Proposed laws first go to a _____ committee for review.

   a. standing   b. conference   c. joint

3. Committees made up of members of both Houses of Congress are called _____ .

   a. special   b. standing   c. joint

4. As Chief Legislator, the President must sign a _____ into law.

   a. veto   b. bill   c. draft

5. Select committees usually last for only one _____ .

   a. year   b. term   c. election

6. Select committees are also called _____ committees.

   a. special   b. civil rights   c. joint

7. A _____ is set up when a committee has too much to do.

   a. special committee   b. judiciary   c. subcommittee

8. The chair of a committee belongs to the _____ party.

   a. President's   b. majority   c. minority

9. The order of business for the House of Representatives is governed by the _____ committee.

   a. rules   b. ethics   c. judiciary

10. The _____ committee deals with impeachments and amendments.

   a. standing   b. joint   c. judiciary

Lawmaking in Congress

Why do you think Congress has had a difficult time passing a term-limit bill?_____

_____

_____

_____

_____

Answer each of the following questions in a complete sentence.

1. Where do ideas for new laws come from? _____

_____

2. What types of concerns may bills address? _____

_____

3. What is a public bill? _____

_____

4. What is a private bill? _____

_____

5. How long does it take for a bill to become a law? _____

_____

6. What happens when a committee tables a bill? _____

_____

7. What is the effect of adding an amendment to a bill? _____

_____

8. Why do some bills pass quickly and others take a whole session to pass? _____

_____

9. Why didn't S.272 become a law? _____

_____

10. Why wasn't H.J.2 sent to the Senate for study? _____

_____

FOCUS

Why was only "he" used when Article I Section 7 of the Constitution was written? _____

_____

_____

_____

_____

A Put the steps in making a law in the correct order below.

writing a draft
signing the bill into law
showing a need for a new law
hearing on the bill

e. standing committee
f. bill sent to the President
g. Rules Committee
h. Congress votes on bill

_____

4. _____

7. _____

_____

5. _____

8. _____

_____

6. _____

B Read the paragraph below. Then rewrite the paragraph in your own words on the lines provided.

Article I Section 7
United States Constitution

ery bill which shall have passed the House of Representatives and the Senate, shall, before it becomes law, be
sented to the President of the United States; if he approves he shall sign it, but if not he shall return it, with
objections to that house in which it shall have originated, who shall enter the objections at large on their
rnal, and proceed to reconsider it."

_____

_____

_____

_____

_____

_____

FOCUS

Give an example of the type of case heard in a U.S. District Court. _____

_____

_____

_____

_____

Answer each of the following questions in a complete sentence.

1. What is the purpose of district courts? _____

_____

2. Where are district courts found? _____

_____

3. Who appoints federal judges? _____

_____

4. How long do federal judges serve? _____

_____

5. What is a criminal case? _____

_____

6. What is a civil case? _____

_____

7. How many district courts are there? _____

_____

8. How many judges preside over each district court? _____

_____

9. What does the 5th Amendment say? _____

_____

10. What does the 6th Amendment say? _____

_____

FOCUS

What do you think should be done about the illegal drug trade in the United States? _____

_____

_____

_____

_____

Use the Data Bank to find out which states and territories are in each of the U.S. Courts of Appeals districts. Show each district on the map.

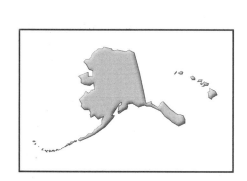

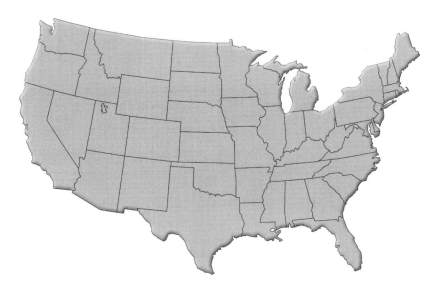

Match each court in **Column B** with its description in **Column A**. Write the correct letter in the space provided.

Column A

_____ 1. hears court cases on tax disputes

_____ 2. reviews court decisions on veterans rights

_____ 3. hears cases about money claims against the U.S.

_____ 4. hears appeals from the U.S. District Courts

_____ 5. hears military appeals

Column B

a. U.S. Claims Court

b. U.S. Court of Military Appeals

c. U.S. Tax Court

d. U.S. Court of Veterans Appeals

e. U.S. Courts of Appeals

FOCUS

Why do you think the framers of the Constitution decided that a Supreme Court justice could serve for life? _____

_____

_____

_____

_____

A Read each statement. If the statement is a fact, write **F** on the line. Write **O** on the line if the statement is an opinion.

_____ 1. The U.S. Supreme Court is the highest federal court.

_____ 2. The U.S. Supreme Court should have the power to strike down state laws.

_____ 3. The U.S. Supreme Court has original jurisdiction in disputes between states.

_____ 4. Some cases can be appealed to the U.S. Supreme Court.

_____ 5. Justices of the U.S. Supreme Court serve for life.

_____ 6. It is good that U.S. Supreme Court Justices are appointed by the President.

_____ 7. Federal laws would be fairer if the U.S. Supreme Court ruled on every law.

_____ 8. *Marbury v. Madison* was the most important ruling of the U.S. Supreme Court.

B Write a paragraph about the following statement. Begin or end your paragraph with a main idea sentence. Give examples.

Explain the difference between original jurisdiction and appellate jurisdiction. Give examples, too.

_____

_____

_____

_____

_____

_____

FOCUS

Write a majority and a minority opinion for a case in Lesson 43.

_____

_____

_____

_____

Use the Important Events in Government Time Line or _index_ of your book to find the year each of the   following events took place. Write the date after each event. Then write the number of each event on the timeline below.

Weeks v. _the United States_ _____

Plessy v. _Ferguson_ _____

The Dred Scott decision _____

The Nineteenth Amendment_____

Black Code laws _____

Brown v. _Board of Education of Topeka_
_____

7. The Bill of Rights is added to the   ___
   Constitution _____

8. The Twenty-sixth Amendment   __
   _____

9. The Fifteenth Amendment _____

10. Indian Removal Act _____

11. Americans with Disabilities Act passed
    _____

1750	1800	1850	1900	1950	2000

Use the events on the time line to complete the following lists.

nts For Civil Rights

_____

_____

_____

_____

_____

Events Against Civil Rights

1._____

2._____

3._____

4._____

FOCUS

Do you agree with the Supreme Court ruling in favor of the Crow Tribe? Explain. _____

_____

_____

_____

_____

A Use the information in Lesson 44 to write what happened in Montana after each of the following dates.

1743 _____

1807 _____

1851 _____

1863 _____

1864 _____

1866 _____

1882 _____

1960 _____

1982 _____

1985 _____

B Write two facts from Lesson 44. Then write two opinions.

Fact	Opinion
1._____	1._____
_____	_____
_____	_____
2._____	2._____
_____	_____
_____	_____

The Checking Power of the President

FOCUS

Why is it difficult to override the President's veto? _____

_____

_____

_____

_____

A Answer each of the following questions in a complete sentence.

What does "balancing power in government" mean? _____

_____

How does "separation of power" work? _____

_____

What happens if the Senate overrides the President's veto?_____

_____

How is an *executive order* different from a *bill*? _____

_____

B Read each statement. If the statement is true, write **T** on the line. Write **F** if the statement is false.

_____ 1. The checking power of Congress helps to balance the powers of the Executive Branch.

_____ 2. It takes only a simple majority in the Senate to override a President's veto.

_____ 3. The President has the power to grant pardons and amnesty.

_____ 4. Executive orders do not have to agree with the Constitution.

C Two statements above are false. Rewrite the false statements to make them true.

_____

_____

_____

_____

FOCUS

Which checking power of Congress do you think is most important? _____

_____

_____

_____

_____

A Use the information from Lesson 46 to explain how Congress overrides a veto.

How Congress Overrides a Veto

_____

_____

_____

_____

_____

_____

_____

_____

_____

B Answer each of the following questions in a complete sentence.

1. How is the War Powers Act a checking power over the President? _____

_____

2. How did the 16th Amendment check the power of the Supreme Court? _____

_____

3. What does "pack the court" mean? _____

_____

FOCUS

How does judicial review act as a check on Congress and on the Executive Branch? _____

_____

_____

_____

_____

A Read and study this chart. Use it to help you complete the table below.

System of Checks and Balances

Executive Branch

The President carries out the law

Judicial Branch

The Courts interpret the law

Legislative Branch

Congress makes the law

B Read each action in the first column of the table. In the second column, write the name of the branch of government that checks each action described. In the last column, write the name of the branch that was checked.

Action	Checking Branch	Branch Checked
. Roosevelt tries to add more Justices to the Supreme Court.		
. Congress passes the Income Tax Law in 1894.		
. President Johnson vetoes the Civil Rights Act of 1865.		
. Congress passes the Fourteenth Amendment.		
. Congress passes the War Powers Act in 1973.		
. President Ford gives former President Nixon a full pardon.		

The Checking Power of the People

FOCUS

In what ways can the people check the power of Congress? __

_____

_____

_____

_____

A List six checking powers of the people.

1. _____   4. _____

2. _____   5. _____

3. _____   6. _____

B Use the words in the box to complete each sentence. You will not use all the words.

checks and balances	judicial	approve
voting	appoint	power
override	legislative	veto
executive	amendment	

The Constitution set up a system of (1) _____ for the federal government. This system

is meant to balance (2) _____ between the three branches of government. One check the

Executive Branch has is the use of the (3) _____. Yet the Legislative Branch can check the

power with an (4) _____. The Legislative Branch can also pass an (5)

_____ to the Constitution. This is a way of checking the

(6) _____ Branch.

The President has the power to (7) _____ federal justices. Yet, the Legislative Branch

must (8) _____ each Justice. The people have the final check on the

government. By (9) _____ the people help to keep democracy strong.

Use with Lesson

FOCUS

How are all state constitutions alike? _____

_____

_____

_____

_____

A List the rules that apply to all state constitutions.

_____

_____

_____

_____

_____

_____

B List the main parts of every state constitution.

_____

_____

_____

_____

_____

C Find out when your state was granted statehood. Then write a short history of your area before it became a state.

Title _____

_____

_____

_____

_____

FOCUS

How is the power of government balanced between the federal and state governments? _____

_____

_____

_____

_____

Use Lesson 50 to fill in the outline below. Write one idea on each line.

I. Powers shared by both the federal and state governments

A._____   E._____

B._____   F._____

C._____   G. _____

D._____

II. Powers of state government

A._____   F._____

B._____   G. _____

C._____   H. _____

D._____   I. _____

E._____   J. _____

III. Powers denied to state governments

A. _____

B._____

C._____

IV. Federal powers that come before state powers

A. _____

B._____

C._____

FOCUS

How does line-item veto power allow a governor to take on the role of a legislator? _____

_____

_____

_____

_____

A Circle the letter of the term that best completes each sentence.

The governor is the _____ of the state.

    a. Chief Executive   b. President   c. Ambassador

One power some governors have that President Clinton had for a short time is

    a. the line-item veto   b. judicial review   c. impeachment

Most governors serve _____ -year terms.

    a. six   b. three   c. four

State governments do not have the power to _____ .

    a. pass laws   b. control businesses   c. coin money

The _____ Amendment says that some powers are reserved for the states.

    a. Ninth   b. Tenth   c. Sixteenth

Both the federal government and state governments get their power from the _____ .

    a. U.S. Constitution   b. people   c. President

State governments, like the federal government, balance power among the _____ of government.

    a. branches   b. executive   c. state departments

Some governors have the power to _____ .

    a. grant pardons   b. elect judges   c. amend the state constitution

B Answer the following question in a complete sentence.

Do you think state officials should be elected or appointed. Why?

_____

_____

The State Legislative Branch

FOCUS

Why must state laws agree with the U. S. Constitution?_____

_____

_____

_____

_____

A   Explain how making state laws is the same as making federal laws.

_____

_____

_____

_____

B   Use reference books or the Internet to fill in the information about your state in the spaces.

Name of House

Upper House _____

Lower House _____

Number of Representatives from each political party

Republican_____

Democratic_____

Governor

Number of Representatives

Upper House _____

Lower House _____

Name _____

Political party_____

Length of term _____

Other

Number of my district_____

Name of my state senator _____

Name of my state representative _____

Length of legislative session _____

Number of my senate district_____

Number of my house/assembly district_____

FOCUS

Do you feel a jury can help a person get a fairer trial? Explain.

_____

_____

_____

_____

_____

A Read each statement. Write **T** on the line if the statement is true. Write **F** if the statement is false.

_____ 1. All state courts use a jury.

_____ 2. The United States Constitution calls for trial by jury.

_____ 3. The United States Courts of Appeals use a jury.

_____ 4. Some state cases may be appealed to the United States Supreme Court.

_____ 5. Trial courts are set up so there is one for each city.

_____ 6. Trial courts have original jurisdiction.

_____ 7. The Supreme Court can change a federal law.

_____ 8. Both U.S. Supreme Court Justices and state supreme court justices may serve for life.

_____ 9. Grand juries are used to decide if someone should be charged with a crime.

B Rewrite each false statement to make it true.

_____

_____

_____

_____

_____

_____

_____

_____

FOCUS

How is zoning an important power of county government?

_____
_____
_____
_____
_____

A Use the information in Lesson 54 to fill in the following lists.

1. List four legislative powers of county government

   a._____   b._____

   c._____   d._____

2. List three executive powers of county government

   a._____   b._____

   c._____

3. List three judicial powers of county government.

   a._____   b._____

   c._____

B Write a sentence using each of the following words.

1. borough   _____

   _____

2. parish   _____

   _____

3. metropolitan   _____

   _____

4. ordinance   _____

   _____

5. zoning   _____

FOCUS

How are committees a part of local, state, and federal government? _____

_____

_____

_____

_____

Use the information in Lessons 49-55 to answer the following questions. Use complete sentences.

How are the roles of county and state officials alike? _____

_____

_____

How are county courts a part of the state court system? _____

_____

_____

What is the difference between a trial jury and a grand jury? _____

_____

_____

How are the executive powers of state and county governments alike? _____

_____

_____

How are the legislative powers of state and county government alike? _____

_____

_____

What kinds of services do you feel are most important for state and local governments to provide? _____

_____

_____

Do you live in a county, parish, or borough? What is its name? _____

_____

FOCUS

Do you think a mayor should have strong or weak executive powers? Explain your answer. _____

_____

_____

_____

Circle the letter of the word or term that best completes each sentence.

1. The most common form of city government is the _____ government.

   a. city manager   b. commission   c. mayor-council

2. The _____ sets down the power of a city government.

   a. ward   b. charter   c. petition

3. Laws passed and enforced by local governments are _____ .

   a. bills   b. ordinances   c. petitions

4. Local governments have the power to _____ land for a certain use.

   a. zone   b. charter   c. impartial

5. Many state governors have _____ power.

   a. line-item veto   b. home rule   c. ward

6. State _____ divide many states into counties.

   a. charters   b. commissions   c. constitutions

7. State governments may not _____ .

   a. give home rule   b. coin money   c. give charters

8. The _____ Amendment is an example of power denied to the states.

   a. Nineteenth   b. Twenty-fifth   c. Twenty-second

FOCUS

Why do you think some large cities are losing population? ____

_____

_____

_____

_____

_____

A Put the events below in the order in which they happened. Write the numbers from 1-9 in the spaces provided.

____ **a.** 1890   Philadelphia population = 1,047,000

____ **b.** 1930   93 cities have populations over 100,000

____ **c.** 1910   1,042,000 immigrants enter the U.S.

____ **d.** 1750   Philadelphia population = 20,000

____ **e.** 1990   • 200 cities have populations over 100,000
             • U.S. population = 249 million

____ **f.** 1840   84,000 immigrants enter the U.S.

____ **g.** 1980   72% of people live in city-suburbs

____ **h.** 1920   • urban population = 54 million
             • rural population = 51 million

____ **i.** 1790   U.S. population = 4 million

B Use the above dates to make comparisons. For example: In 1790 the United States had a population of 4 million. By 1990, the population had grown to 249 million.

_____

_____

_____

_____

_____

_____

_____

_____

Towns and Villages

FOCUS

What are three things that keep town and village governments strong? _____

_____

_____

_____

_____

A Answer each of the following questions in a complete sentence.

_____

1. How are town meetings an example of a direct democracy? _____

_____

_____

2. What are some local services that town and village governments provide? _____

_____

_____

3. What problems do town and village governments have? _____

_____

_____

B Compare town and village governments.

Town	Village
a. _____	_____
b. _____	_____
c. _____	_____
d. _____	_____

FOCUS

What does balancing the budget mean? Explain. _____

_____

_____

_____

_____

_____

A Use words from Lesson 63 to complete the following paragraph.

The federal budget is made up of two main parts called (1)_____ and

(2)_____. The (3)_____ _____ plans the federal budget.

By the first Monday in (4)_____, the President must give (5)_____ a budget

for the next year. The federal government's (6)_____ _____ begins in

October of each year. Congress studies the budget in the form of an (7)_____ bill. People can

lend the government money by buying U.S. Savings Bonds. The federal government must pay

(8)_____ on all money it borrows.

B Use the graph on page 194 to answer the following questions.

What percent is spent on education?(a)_____ national defense?(b)_____

Which area do you believe is over spent? _____ Why? _____

Which area do you believe should get more federal dollars? _____

Why? _____

Write the percent you think each area should get. Your total must equal 100.

a. space, agriculture, foreign affairs _____

b. national defense _____

c. justice _____

d. environment, housing _____

e. social security _____

f. interest on public debt _____

general government _____

h. health _____

i. education _____

j. transportation _____

k. income security _____

l. other _____

FOCUS

Why does the government want people to buy United States Savings Bonds? _____

_____

_____

_____

_____

A Read each cause. Then write an effect of each cause.

Cause	Effect
1. inflation	1. _____
2. budget deficit	2. _____
3. balanced budget	3. _____
4. the public debt	4. _____
5. surplus of tax dollars	5. _____
6. buying a U.S. Savings Bond	6. _____
7. borrowing money	7. _____
8. raising taxes	8. _____

B Write three facts and three opinions from Lesson 60.

Facts	Opinions
1. _____	1. _____
2. _____	2. _____
3. _____	3. _____

FOCUS

Do you think tariffs encourage or restrict trade? Explain. _____

_____

_____

_____

_____

_____

A Complete each sentence with a word or term from the box.

income tax	balanced budget	inflation
Federal Reserve Board	excise taxes	defense
budget deficit	bonds	direct tax

_____ is the term used to describe the cost of things rising quickly.

People pay _____ on certain items such as cigarettes and alcohol.

The Sixteenth Amendment put into place a federal _____ .

One of the largest budget items in the federal budget is _____ .

When the federal government spends more than it takes in, a _____ results.

People can lend money to the government by buying _____ .

The _____ controls the amount of money banks must keep in reserve.

Income tax paid to the Internal Revenue Service is an example of a _____ .

A _____ shows that money spent is equal to the money taken in.

B Explain the difference between the public debt and a budget deficit.

_____

_____

_____

_____

_____

_____

FOCUS

Not every state uses property taxes to fund education. What other sources of income could be used? _____

_____

_____

_____

_____

A

Match each term in Column B with its meaning in Column A. Write the letter of the correct term on the line provided.

Column A	Column B
_____ 1. money given for a special purpose	a. value
_____ 2. money which can be spent	b. interest
_____ 3. types of income	c. revenue
_____ 4. how much something is worth	d. funds
_____ 5. extra money owed when money is borrowed	e. lottery
_____ 6. game of chance	f. grant

B

Complete the chart. Give at least two examples for each box.

	FEDERAL	STATE
Sources of Revenue		
Expenses		

FOCUS

What local services do you feel should be funded by tax dollars? Explain your choices. _____

_____

_____

_____

A Write a paragraph that answers the question below. Remember to begin or end your paragraph with a main idea sentence.

What are some ways that school systems can improve education without having to increase school costs?

_____

_____

_____

_____

_____

_____

_____

B Write a sentence using each of the following words.

goods _____

_____

excise tax _____

_____

inflation _____

_____

value _____

_____

deficit _____

_____

WORKBOOK ACTIVITY 64

Immigration

FOCUS

Why do people immigrate to the United States? _____

_____

_____

_____

_____

A Each phrase mentions an event in history. Write the effect of the event.

Event

1. potato famine in Ireland

2. poor economy in Germany during the mid-1800s

3. white settlements expand westward

4. 40 million immigrants moved to the United States

5. one million enslaved Africans brought to the U.S. by 1790

1. _____

2. _____

_____

3. _____

4. _____

_____

5. _____

_____

Effect

B Write a sentence using each of the following words.

1. native _____

2. immigrate _____

3. barriers _____

4. melting pot _____

5. mosaic _____

Use with Lesson

FOCUS

Do you feel it is right to ask naturalized citizens to pledge loyalty to the United States? _____

_____

_____

_____

_____

A Use information from Lesson 65 to complete the following paragraphs.

Naturalization allows a person to become a (1) _____ of another country. Naturalized citizens may (2) _____ in local elections. Naturalized citizens have the same (3)_____ as people born in the United States.

A foreign-born person may become a citizen after having lived in the United States for (4)_____ years. Foreign-born children of United States citizens (5)_____ become citizens of the United States. All naturalized citizens pledge to be (6) _____ to the United States.

B Write a **T** before each true statement. Write an **F** before each false statement.

_____ 1. A person may apply for naturalization after living in the United States for one year.

_____ 2. Citizenship is granted to anyone who applies to become a United States citizen.

_____ 3. It is possible for a naturalized United States citizen to lose his or her citizenship.

_____ 4. A naturalized citizen may work in a foreign country without giving up his or her American citizenship.

_____ 5. An INS official may order the loss of citizenship.

C Rewrite each false statement to make it true.

_____

_____

_____

FOCUS

Do you think limits should be placed on immigration? _____

_____

_____

_____

_____

_____

A Explain each of the following laws. Tell what the law was about. Discuss the effect of each law.

1. 1882 Chinese Exclusion Act _____

_____

_____

2. 1864 Contract Labor Law _____

_____

_____

3. 1924 National Origins Act _____

_____

_____

4. 1990 Immigration Act _____

_____

_____

B Write your opinion to the question below.

Do you think the law should allow more immigrants from some countries than from other

countries? Why or why not? _____

_____

_____

_____

_____

_____

FOCUS

What are some ways to get more people active in government? _____

_____

_____

_____

_____

A | Use complete sentences to tell how each of the following groups or actions can affect government.

lobbies _____

_____

voting blocks _____

_____

petitions _____

_____

referendums _____

_____

absentee ballots _____

_____

active citizens _____

_____

B | Write a paragraph that explains how you can be an active citizen in your community.

_____

_____

_____

_____

_____

FOCUS

How do U.S. territories add to the richness of cultures that make up the United States?_____

_____

_____

_____

_____

Place the U.S. territories on the map below. Also fill in the name of the ocean surrounding each territory.

1. The Northern Mariana Islands
2. Guam
3. American Samoa
4. Virgin Islands
5. Puerto Rico
6. Pacific Ocean
7. Atlantic Ocean

Use with Lesson

FOCUS

Why do events that happen in one country affect many other counties in the world? _____

_____

_____

_____

_____

A Explain how events shaped the governments of the following countries.

1. The former Soviet Union _____

_____

_____

2. Hong Kong _____

_____

_____

3. South Africa_____

_____

_____

B Answer each of the following questions in a complete sentence.

How do you think the change in government affected the people of the newly independent countries of the USSR? _____

_____

_____

What kinds of changes would you expect in Hong Kong after it became part of China in 1997? _____

_____

_____

How does a country's economy affect its relations with other countries in the world? _____

_____

_____

FOCUS

What kinds of problems might a country have when its government changes?_____

_____

_____

_____

Write five facts about each lesson in Unit 12. Then write one opinion for each group of facts you listed.

A. Lesson 68 Facts

1. _____

2. _____

3. _____

4. _____

5. _____

A. Your Opinion

_____

_____

_____

_____

_____

B. Lesson 69 Facts

1. _____

2. _____

3. _____

4. _____

5. _____

B. Your Opinion

_____

_____

_____

_____

_____

C. Lesson 70 Facts

1. _____

2. _____

3. _____

4. _____

5. _____

C. Your Opinion

_____

_____

_____

_____

_____

Read the steps in the writing process. Use them to help you as you write an essay.

Writing is a process. Think of writing in steps.
First, you **prewrite,** or plan.
Then, you **draft,** or write.
Next, you **revise,** or fix.
Fourth, you **proofread,** or edit.
Last, you **publish,** or present in final form.

Step 1 Prewrite
List six ideas you could put in your paragraph. Then number your ideas in the order you will write them.

Step 2 Draft
Write your paragraph. Remember to begin with a main idea sentence. This is called your *topic* sentence. Be sure to give your paragraph a title.

Step 3 Revise
Read your paragraph aloud. Do the ideas flow? Do your sentences start and stop as you want them to? Mark your mistakes. Then rewrite your paragraph.

Step 4 Proofread
Are the words spelled correctly? Did you use punctuation correctly? Do your sentences use correct grammar? Mark any mistakes.

Step 5 Publish
Write your paragraph for the third time. This is the final or correct copy that you want to present.

Write an essay about "Foreign Policy." Follow the steps above. Use a separate sheet of paper to write your essay.

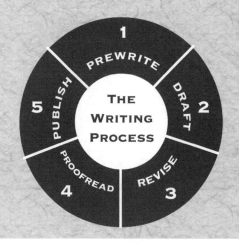

 A Review the steps in the writing process.

Step 1 Prewrite
List six ideas you could put in your paragraph. Then number your ideas in the order you will write them.

Step 2 Draft
Write your paragraph. Remember to begin with a main idea sentence. This is called your *topic* sentence. Be sure to give your paragraph a title.

Step 3 Revise
Read your paragraph aloud. Do the ideas flow? Do your sentences start and stop as you want them to? Mark your mistakes. Then rewrite your paragraph.

Step 4 Proofread
Are the words spelled correctly? Did you use punctuation correctly? Do your sentences use correct grammar? Mark any mistakes.

Step 5 Publish
Write your paragraph for the third time. This is the final or correct copy that you want to present.

 B Write an essay to answer these questions:
(Use the steps in the writing process as you write your essay.)
1. What area of civil rights do you see as a problem in the United States?
2. What law would you like to see passed to address the problem?